I0624011

THEOLOGY

AND

APOLOGETICS

AN EXAMINATION OF HOW AND WHERE
THEY INTERSECT

L. J. ANDERSON

LAMAD PRESS

Published by Lamad Press. PO Box 50785, Billings, MT 59105.

www.lamadpress.com

ISBN 978-1-963291-00-1 (hardback), 978-1-963291-01-8 (paperback), and 978-1-963291-02-5 (eBook)

Book cover by Jenn Anderson

Copy editing and proofreading by Courtney Oppel

First edition 2024

CONTENTS

WHY A BOOK INSTEAD OF A JOURNAL ARTICLE?

Welcome to *Theology and Apologetics: An Examination of How and Where They Intersect.* I want to give some insight into how this book came about and why I chose to take the path I did. This short book was originally written as an article I planned to submit to academic journals. I ended up submitting it to exactly *one* journal before I stopped and thought, "Wait a second, why am I doing this?" You see, ever since I started writing books, I decided I wanted to go the self-publishing route. I like the creative liberty and the potential for higher returns, and, quite frankly, I did not want someone else telling me whether I could publish something. Also, a well-written and well-edited self-published book is as high quality as a traditionally published book. Gone are the days when someone can easily tell a self-published book from a traditionally published book. These are things I considered when making the decision to self-publish, which brings us back to this book.

After I submitted this article to a journal, I realized that I had even more reservations about publishing through journals than I do with traditional book publishers. For one thing, journals have a monopoly on academic, peer-reviewed writing. If you want your writing to be instantly regarded as reputable, you pretty much *have* to get published in a well-respected journal. Additionally, this is almost the only way to get something of journal-article length widely available in academic libraries. Publishing to a website is simply not going to cut it. However, self-published books, when done correctly, are available to every library, just like traditionally published books. Thus, one *should* be able to get journal articles into academic libraries without going through a journal by publishing it in book format.

Another contention I have with journals is that they often profit significantly from academics' work while the academics themselves get *nothing*. It can be argued that academics gain the prestige needed to get a teaching or research position and eventually earn tenure. However, as a Christian theologian, I believe that "The laborer deserves his wages" (1 Timothy 5:18). The amount of time and effort an academic puts into writing a journal article is quite significant, yet they gain nothing, at least monetarily, in return. In some cases, the authors of the articles have to *pay* to get published in a journal! And after that, the author receives zero monetary return. I would argue that this is a borderline predatory practice, especially since journals hold the monopoly on peer-reviewed, academic writing. At least publishing through a traditional book publisher offers authors the potential for financial returns.

Now, I am not all about the money. I am in the writing game to make a difference in the lives of fellow Christians regardless of their academic background. That said, I do think there is a better way than the traditional path, one that can help me support my family and allow me to devote significant time to doing original research and writing while also giving my writing a chance to be read and reviewed at the academic level. Self-publishing allows writers to publish books of any length and make them available everywhere traditionally published books are available. This means that I can get my book into academic libraries where it has a chance of being engaged at the scholarly level. It allows for the potential of organic peer review. Admittedly, the lack of a double-blind peer review prior to publication is the biggest downside to this method of publication, yet it is only *after* articles and books are published that the true peer review begins. Of course, a traditionally published book has instant name-brand recognition; however, that does not mean the book is good or that it presents solid research. Likewise, just because a journal article is peer-reviewed does not mean that the article is inherently better than one that has not been peer-reviewed.

This book, and the others I hope to publish the same way, exists primarily as an experiment to see if this method of publishing original research is as viable as it seems to be on paper. Academia can be a slow-moving beast. It does not like changing how things are done. That said, self-publishing has proven itself to be an effective alternative to traditional publishing outside of academia provided that one is willing to put in the time, money, and effort to make a solid product. Now is the time for testing whether the same can be said for academic writing.

Ultimately, I hope that this experiment will result in greater access to original research and will one day be viewed as a legitimate way for academic researchers to publish their findings and hopefully see monetary returns for their time and effort.

While I would love for this concept to catch on in the academic world, this book's true goal is to bring people closer to Christ. In pursuit of that goal, I pray you will find value in this book and that God will draw you to himself. Additionally, I pray that he will use this work to make you more effective in practicing theology and apologetics, regardless of your academic background.

ABSTRACT

Theology and Apologetics delves into the disciplines of theology and apologetics and how they are traditionally viewed as separate from each other, with apologetics being a rather narrow field. On the other hand, theology is such a broad term that it is regularly broken down into subcategories like pastoral theology, or even specific theologies, like eschatology. This book demonstrates that the field of apologetics is much broader than is typically accepted and should be applied across the gamut of theology.

Chapter 1

Setting the Stage

Theology and apologetics are typically viewed as two very different disciplines. Is this assumption accurate, though? Unfortunately, this question is not easily answered. The typical treatment of apologetics *is* very different from the typical treatment of theology. Traditionally, apologetics deals with making a defense for one's faith and training other Christians to do the same. For example, after noting that the term "apologetics" comes from the Greek ἀπολογία meaning "defense," Christian philosophers Paul Gould, Travis Dickenson, and R. Keith Loftin define apologetics as "*an attempt to remove obstacles or doubts to, as well as offer positive reasons for, believing that Christianity is true and satisfying*" (italics in original).[1] They, and others who ascribe to this definition, then proceed to defend Christianity against other religions and philosophies. Theology, on the other hand, is focused on what Scripture says, and what the church believes, about God.[2]

Based on these distinctives, one can easily see that there appears to be a big gap between theology and apologetics. However, unlike what is traditionally believed about how these two disciplines function, there is a lot of overlap between them. This can most readily be seen in a reduction of what apologetics is. This book seeks to compare theology and apologetics in Scripture with how they are viewed contemporarily, and to demonstrate that the discipline of apologetics aligns with theology well and should be applied across the gamut of theology.

Setting the Stage

Before beginning, there is an exceedingly important point to discuss. When researching a topic that Scripture teaches,

---

1. Paul Gould, Travis Dickenson, and R. Keith Loftin, *Stand Firm: Apologetics and the Brilliance of the Gospel* (Nashville, TN: B&H Academic, 2018), 2.

2. Johannes Zachhuber, "What is Theology? Historical and Systematic Reflections," *International Journal for the Study of the Christian Church*, 21, no. 3-4, (December 2021): 198-99. https://doi.org/10.1080/1474225X.2021.2006107.

one *must* look beyond merely the use of specific words. Often, Scripture addresses a concept without using a specific word that embodies that concept. If one were to pull only from the passages that have that word, one would necessarily have a skewed view of what Scripture says about that topic. In some cases, Scripture might *never* use a word but that does not mean it is not addressed. One very common example of this is the Trinity. Investigating what the Bible says about the Trinity by focusing only on the times that it discusses the word "trinity" would lead the reader to conclude that the doctrine of the Trinity is not remotely biblical. The word itself is never found in Scripture, but the *concept* is. This is also true of theology and, to a lesser degree, apologetics. Most Christians and scholars are aware of this, but it bears repeating as it is an integral perspective necessary for understanding the content of this book.

CHAPTER 2

CONTEMPORARY AND BIBLICAL THEOLOGY

C ONTEMPORARY THEOLOGY IS AN interesting beast. Theology is such a broad term that it is regularly broken down into distinct "types" (e.g., systematic, biblical, and historical theology).[1] Beyond that, it is broken down even *further* into divisions of theology like Christology, bibliology, eschatology, et cetera. Typically, when a book or article addresses theology, it either provides an overview of the various divisions, like Wayne Grudem's *Systematic Theology*, or dives headlong into a specific division, as in Christopher R. J. Holmes's *The Holy Spirit*. The modern method of education emphasizes the latter. PhD candidates must pick a very narrow problem to research and solve. Although this is excellent for producing

---

1. Daniel L. Akin, David S. Dockery, Nathan A. Finn, and Christopher W. Morgan, eds., chapters 8-12 in *A Handbook of Theology* (Nashville, TN: B&H Publishing Group, 2023).

original research that solves a problem in one particular field, it also has the potential to create other problems. This model produces experts in a very narrow field, and essentially pigeon-holes them into a myopic area of expertise. Kevin Vanhoozer notes, "Most scholars are specialists who know a lot about a little, but are tongue tied when it comes to the big questions."[2] One example of this tendency can be seen in the life of the late biblical scholar Michael Heiser. While he did teach outside of what his dissertation addressed, he spent the majority of his life and ministry writing and teaching around the same subject as his dissertation.[3] Similarly, professors are often hired for their expertise in a specific area (e.g., New Testament) and then expected to research and publish work in that area only. Biblically and historically, theologians did not have this narrow focus. Theologian Peter J. Leithart writes, "Academic biblical studies has institutionalized this fragmentation with its departments

---

2. Todd Wilson and Gerald Hiestand, eds, *Becoming a Pastor Theologian: New Possibilities for Church Leadership* (Downers Grove, IL: InterVarsity Press, 2016), 43-44.

3. His dissertation is titled "The Divine Council in Late Canonical and Non-Canonical Second Temple Jewish Literature."

of Old and New Testament. But the fragmented Enlighten-
ment Bible is not the Bible of the church. Pastors and pastor
theologians must learn (again) to read and study the Bible as a
single book."[4] There absolutely is value in knowing a lot about
a very narrow subject; however, when it comes to God and his
Word, having an emphasis on being more generalist is equally
valuable. Being highly specialized should not come at the cost
of developing a bad method of theology, which leads to this
question: How did people in the Bible do theology?

Theology Versus Theology Applied

Before answering the above question, it makes sense to look
more into the term "theology." This term does not appear in
any form in the Bible except when separated from its com-
pound form, in which case both θεός and λόγος can be found
in abundance.[5] This means that one must broaden their search
of Scripture to come up with a good view of what it teaches
on theology. It is best to begin with a simple definition of what

---

4. Wilson and Hiestand, eds, *Becoming a Pastor Theologian*, 12-13.

5. These are the two Greek words that form the word "theology." Individually,
θεός occurs in Scripture over thirteen hundred times and λόγος occurs over three
hundred times.

theology is. *Merriam-Webster's Dictionary* defines theology as "the study of religious faith, practice, and experience *especially*: the study of God and of God's relation to the world." This last part happens to be what the author of this book believes theology should be defined as. This definition allows one to see that Scripture itself determines what theology is. The God-breathed Scriptures, as Paul mentioned in 2 Timothy 3:16, tell us about who God is, how he relates to mankind and the world, and how he expects mankind to relate to him. The Bible is *the* textbook on theology. All other theology books pale in comparison; and, if they do not faithfully teach the Bible itself, they have utterly failed in illuminating God.

The simple definition also helps us avoid one of the major pitfalls of theology, which is the tendency to study God but never apply what one has learned. Anyone who makes a practice of studying God will quickly realize that he expects them to *follow* him. It is easy to focus on one aspect of theology so much that one becomes an expert on the theory but fails to apply the knowledge gained. This is a fundamental failure in understanding the purpose of doing theology. Theology should always have the end goal of obedience and deepening one's relationship with the one true God. Professor and former pastor John Hammett states, "Doctrine should govern and guide practice."[6] Anytime doctrine is studied and systematized, it should be applied to one's life. Without that application, the student misses the whole point of learning. Additionally, theologians have often been accused of over-complicating things so that theology is out of reach of lay Christians and not particularly applicable or valuable to them. Theology and religion professors Jonathan M. Womack and Jerry Pillay show how this is the case in South Africa. In a journal article they co-wrote, they argue that theology is something that every Christian should partake in but, at least in South Africa, that is not the case, stating, "The 'study of God', an enterprise every Christian believer partakes in, has been institutionalized and specialized making the 'theologian' an exclusive title, detached from the everyday reality."[7] While this is specifically talking about South Africa, it also applies to the United States—though theologians tend to be further along

---

6. John S. Hammett, *Biblical Foundations for Baptist Churches: A Contemporary Ecclesiology* (Grand Rapids, MI: Kregel Publications, 2005), 67.

7. Jonathan M. Womack and Jerry Pillay, "From the Tower to the Pews: A Call for Academic Theology to Re-Engage with the Local Context," *Hervormde Teologiese Studies* 75, no. 4 (2019): 1.

in rectifying this disconnect here. Theology must be done at all levels of Christianity, and it must be done in a way that drives people to action rather than mere words.

It can be argued that even though theology is already a huge field and needs to be broken down into different areas and divisions, contemporarily it is too narrow for the dictionary definition above. The challenge with the simple definition of theology is that it makes *anything* that discusses God and how he interacts with his creation into theology. Since the Bible is God's Word revealed to humans, any study done on it is, by definition, theology. Additionally, using reason to argue for the God of the Bible and against other gods or philosophies necessitates studying God and how he interacts with creation which, again, is theology. Thus, what one might normally call biblical studies, apologetics, homiletics, et cetera, are really just theology or theology applied. For example, apologetics can faithfully be argued as being theology applied because it seeks to defend God and his Word. One must necessarily be a theologian first in order to accurately and faithfully defend God. It is only from one's knowledge of God, gained through the study of God, that one can properly defend God.

Theology in Scripture

Despite *theology* never appearing in Scripture, Paul is said to have been "the first and greatest Christian theologian" and rightly so.[8] Paul's life and ministry oozed theology. That said, despite attempts to find a metanarrative of Paul's theology, he remains more of a generalist. He willingly and readily addressed anything and everything surrounding God and his Word, from marriage, to food sacrificed to idols, to Israel, to salvation, to sin, to end times, and many more areas. Similarly, the other writers of the New Testament also demonstrate this generalist approach to theology. They all addressed whatever problems were pertinent to the early church. Paul had to keep coming back to the idea that salvation is by grace through faith precisely because it kept cropping up as an issue for debate in the early church. His writings would be devoid of this particular area of theology if the early church did not struggle so significantly with it since his letters were pastoral and occasional in nature.[9]

---

8. James D. G. Dunn, *The Theology of Paul the Apostle* (Grand Rapids, MI: Wm. B. Eerdmans Publishing, 2006), 1.

9. Walter Elwell and Robert Yarbrough, *Encountering the New Testament: A Historical and Theological Survey* (Grand Rapids, MI: Baker Academic, 2013), 238.

CHAPTER 3

CONTEMPORARY AND BIBLICAL APOLOGETICS

U NLIKE CONTEMPORARY THEOLOGY, WHICH encompasses a wide range of topics, contemporary apologetics is typically a rather narrow field of study. When arguing for a return to original (biblical and early church) apologetics, Christian apologist Stuart Nicolson writes, "Original apologetics, according to Scripture, especially the clear Petrine call for all the faithful to be prepared to respond to others' questions and challenges in a Christian manner, was quite unlike the way apologetics later developed, which was far narrower: more elite, intellectual, and often clerical."[1] This is true of apologetics today—many view it as only something select theologians can do.

---

1. Stuart Nicolson, "Original Apologetics," *Theology and Philosophy of Education* 2, no. 2 (December 2023): 4.

Many church congregants, though fascinated by apologetics, rarely engage in it themselves. But Nicolson does not take this idea far enough. Contemporary apologetics, and much of historical apologetics, is too narrowly defined for what is actually seen through logic and Scripture. Most books on apologetics are likely to address similar topics and almost exclusively focus on defending Christianity against contrary worldviews.[2] This restrictive agenda is problematic.

One particular book demonstrates the contemporary view of apologetics quite well. In *Five Views on Apologetics*, edited by Steven B. Cowan and William Lane Craig, five scholars debate over *methods* of apologetics. Cowan, in the introduction, says, "Although apologists agree on the basic definition and goals of apologetics, they can differ significantly on the proper *methodology* of apologetics."[3] The commonly agreed-upon definition

---

2. "Almost exclusively" because on rare occasions one will run into a non-typical example of apologetics in one of these books. For an example see Khaldoun A. Sweis and Chad V. Meister's *Christian Apologetics: An Anthology of Primary Sources* which discusses "The Trinity" in Part 3 of the book. This is a non-typical chapter in an apologetics book that is normally in the realm of theology.

3. Steven B. Cowan and William Lane Craig, eds., *Five Views on Apologetics* (Grand Rapids, MI: Zondervan, 2000), 8.

and goals of apologetics are laid out as follows: It is defined as "defending, or making a case for, the truth of the Christian faith" and is typically used to "bolster the faith of Christian believers" and "aid in the task of evangelism."[4] There is an impressive unity regarding the concept of apologetics among the different methodologies despite significant, and often sharp, disagreement on the methods themselves.[5]

Whereas contemporary theology is broken down into different types and divisions, apologetics is mostly broken down into extremely broad topics, such as whether God exists, or narrow topics, such as an ontological argument. As noted above, apologetics is typically used as an aid to evangelism or to bolster a Christian's faith. This is almost a universal view among apologists and theologians. Should apologetics be this narrow? Scripture argues that it should not.

Apologetics in Scripture

In order to have an accurate view of how Scripture teaches the discipline of apologetics, it is crucial to engage with both the Old and New Testaments.

---

4. Ibid., 8.

5. Ibid., 7.

New Testament

To begin with, the use of the word ἀπολογία in Scripture
needs to be dissected. The word occurs eight times in the New
Testament. As noted above, this word means "defense," however, it has a bit more nuance than that. In his defense of reason
and the mind in the life of Christians, philosophy professor J.
P. Moreland gives an example of ἀπολογία as "offering positive
arguments for and responding to negative arguments against
your position in a courtroom."[6] He then points out that this
is exactly how the Apostle Paul did evangelism. He defended
his position with positive arguments and responded to negative arguments. For this book, however, the question is: Does
Scripture limit this word to evangelistic uses only? To answer
this question, each of the eight scriptural uses of ἀπολογία will
be examined.

The most common Scripture used to discuss apologetics is
a good place to start. First Peter 3:15 says, "But in your hearts
honor Christ the Lord as holy, always being prepared to make
a defense to anyone who asks you for a reason for the hope

---

6. J. P. Moreland, *Love the Lord Your God with All Your Mind: The Role of Reason
in the Life of the Soul* (Colorado Springs, CO: NavPress, 2012), 54.

that is in you; yet do it with gentleness and respect." This verse, especially considering its context, is clearly geared toward evangelism and thus does not play much of a role in this discussion. Similarly, Acts 22:1, Acts 25:16, Philippians 1:7, Philippians 1:16, and 2 Timothy 4:16 are all examples of ἀπολογία being used regarding making a defense for the gospel.

That still leaves two uses of the word in 1 Corinthians 9:3 and 2 Corinthians 7:11. The former says, "This is my defense to those who would examine me." Whereas the previous six verses were solidly in the realm of evangelism, this verse, when taking the context into consideration, is focused on Paul's defense of himself and his teaching to those who are already followers of Jesus. Likewise, 2 Corinthians 7:11 says, "For see what earnestness this godly grief has produced in you, *but also what eagerness to clear yourselves*, what indignation, what fear, what longing, what zeal, what punishment! At every point you have proved yourselves innocent in the matter" (emphasis added). The context of this verse can be found in verse 1 which says, "Since we have these promises, beloved, let us cleanse ourselves from every defilement of body and spirit, bringing holiness to completion in the fear of God." The Corinthian believers were zealous in clearing themselves and proving themselves innocent.

Again, this is not focused on evangelism. Thus, merely the use of the word ἀπολογία in Scripture argues that there is more to the term than defending the gospel itself and the existence of God to non-believers.

Beyond the specific uses of ἀπολογία, one can see that the *act* of making a defense is *exceedingly* common in Scripture. While ἀπολογία is only used eight times, the concept of "making a defense" is literally what almost every letter of the New Testament *is*. Nearly every Epistle has some level of emphasis on defending the faith, or certain aspects of it, primarily from attacks from within the church rather than from the outside. This happens outside of the Epistles as well. One example of this is Paul's discussion with the Ephesian elders in Acts 20:29-31 which says, "I know that after my departure fierce wolves will come in among you, not sparing the flock; and from among your own selves will arise men speaking twisted things, to draw away the disciples after them. Therefore be alert, remembering that for three years I did not cease night or day to admonish every one with tears." Paul spent three years warning the Ephesians night and day because he knew that "fierce wolves" would arise from among the elders who would mislead the congregation. This was, fundamentally, a preemptive defense that he laid out for years with tears because of the passion that he had for this defense.

Jesus, likewise, often practiced apologetics. For example, in Mark 12:28-34, Jesus was confronted by an expert of the Law who was trying to trick him into saying that one specific commandment was more important than all the others. However, Jesus defended himself extremely well. Not only did he give the expert of the Law an answer, but he did so in a way that this man could not catch him, and "from then on no one dared ask him any more questions" (Mark 12:34). This is a classic example of apologetics being done and, as anyone who has spent time reading the Gospels knows, Jesus *regularly* did things like this.

But what about the Epistles? It was argued earlier that they were typically written as a defense, at least on some level. An excellent example of this can be found in Galatians. The entire book of Galatians is Paul's defense of the gospel to those who already knew the gospel. He argued vehemently that salvation is by grace through faith and that falling back into salvation via works or the Jewish identity is a fall from grace (Galatians 5:4). He goes so far as to say that if he, or even an angel, were to bring them a gospel other than that which they had received, that person was to be anathematized (Galatians 1:8). Paul was practicing apologetics here! He was defending the faith against an attack from *within* the church. Likewise, 1 Corinthians has Paul making a defense for such things as proper sexual relations, the body of Christ, the day of the Lord, love, and spiritual gifts, to name a few. Any time one of the Epistles corrects or warns the readers of something, it can rightly be defined as an apologetic defense. Since the Epistles were written for specific audiences in specific situations, often with the express purpose of correction or warning, they are apologetic in nature.

Old Testament

The defenses found in the New Testament regularly pull from the Old Testament. However, as has been noted by theologian Siegbert Riecker in his book *The Old Testament Basis of Christian Apologetics: A Biblical-Theological Survey*, the Old Testament is almost completely ignored as a rationale for the discipline of apologetics.[7] The foundation of everything in the New Testament comes from the Old. Thus, the Old Testament cannot and should not be ignored on any topic of Scripture. The New Testament writers were keenly aware of this, as can be

---

7. Siegbert Riecker, *The Old Testament Basis of Christian Apologetics: A Biblical-Theological Survey* (Eugene, OR: Wipf and Stock Publishers, 2018), xiii.

seen with their regular references to the Old Testament. Even Paul's famed defense for salvation through faith in Galatians 3:6-14 is based not in his own theology, but rather in the Old Testament pulling from the life of Abraham and other areas of the Hebrew Scriptures. So, what does the Old Testament provide in regard to a rationale for the discipline of apologetics?

One significant example of apologetics in the Old Testament is the book of Job. In it, God demonstrates and defends his nature and authority. Beyond that though, Job and his friends engage in a lengthy debate over Job's sinlessness or lack thereof. His friends argued with him, saying, "Remember: who that was innocent ever perished? Or where were the upright cut off?" (Job 4:7). Their essential argument was that Job *must* have some sin that he does not know of. Job defends himself by proclaiming that God does not punish anyone for secret sins and then rightfully proclaims his innocence. Unfortunately, while he was correct in both regards, he eventually *did* sin by saying that God must have made some mistake. He said, "But I would speak to the Almighty, and I desire to argue my case with God" (Job 13:3). Job wished to *make a defense* before God. God not only heard his defense, but defended *himself* against Job. He comes before Job in Job 38-41 and defends his knowledge and power as being infinitely more than Job could even dream of for himself. He challenges Job to prove his knowledge. Job responds by shutting up and repenting. This is a fantastic example of apologetics within the Old Testament.

One of the challenges of finding examples of apologetics in the Old Testament is the fact that atheists were rare in Old Testament times.[8] Pretty much everyone believed in God, a god, or gods. A significant portion of contemporary apologetics is focused on demonstrating that God is the most reasonable answer for the origins of the universe, but this concept was almost universally held in the ancient world.[9] Thus, Old Testament writers had no need to make these arguments. Instead, the defense that they focused on was in demonstrating that Yahweh is the one true God—typically by comparing Yahweh with false gods. God himself provides one of the best examples of this in Isaiah 44:9-20. Another example of this specific apologetic

---

8. Ramm Bernard, "The Apologetic of the Old Testament: The Basis of a Biblical and Christian Apologetic," *Bulletin of the Evangelical Theological Society* 1.4 (Fall 1958), 15.

9. At least some version of a higher power was known to have created everything, even if it was not the God of the Bible.

focus can be seen in the passage where Elijah challenges the prophets of Ba'al in 1 Kings 18. Nearly all of the books of the Old Testament include some level of apologetic argument focused on demonstrating that Yahweh is the one true God and idols are nothing.[10]

---

10. See Bernard's "The Apologetic of the Old Testament" and Riecker's *The Old Testament Basis of Christian Apologetics* for a more robust discussion on the apologetic arguments of the Old Testament.

CHAPTER 4

THE POINT OF INTERSECTION

EVEN IF ONE REJECTS the notion argued earlier that apologetics and similar disciplines are simply theology applied, there is still substantial evidence that suggests that apologetics and theology are much more closely intertwined than most people realize. Though it is the author's belief that disciplines like apologetics fit comfortably under the roof of theology, for the sake of argument he is going to argue the point of intersection between theology and apologetics as if that is not his belief.

Christian theology focuses on trying to correctly understand God and how he interacts with the world. One of the common and important understandings that comes out of theology is God's unchangeability. Scripture claims this and philosophy tends to agree with the claim.[1] Additionally, God has revealed himself through his Word so that humans can know him. However, humans are fallible. Our understanding of who God is and how he relates to and interacts with creation can be faulty. This is where apologetics comes in. Christians are to defend theology through God's Word. Sometimes this is done amid nonbelievers as traditional apologetics espouses, but many times it is done Christian-to-Christian, as "iron sharpens iron" (Proverbs 27:17) to align one another closer to God and his Word—the goal of theology. Thus, apologetics and theology intersect whenever a defense of any kind is needed; and in theology, it is almost *always* needed to defend the correct teaching about God. Just as the Bible regularly shows apologetics in practice, theologians also engage with apologetics anytime they argue for, or against, a particular doctrine. This book is itself a demonstration of apologetics.

Overall, it is better to view apologetics as a *technique* rather than a distinct *area* of theology. It is the technique, skill, or art of giving a defense for something. To be sure, traditional apolo-

---

1. John S. Feinberg, *No One Like Him: The Doctrine of God* (Wheaton, IL: Crossway, 2001), 800.

getics is a distinct discipline and likely should *remain* a distinct discipline; however, it is too narrow of a discipline to properly cover what apologetics in general covers, or at least should cover, just as the term "theology" should not be limited to theology proper. Apologetics should be broken down like theology is. There is apologetics "proper," which fits the traditional view of apologetics (giving a defense for the Christian hope), and there is apologetics in general, which covers every *other* defense. Thus, one could do apologetic theology and be an apologetic theologian.

CHAPTER 5

CONCLUSION AND APPLICATION

DESPITE WHAT MANY BELIEVE, theology and apologetics are much more closely intertwined than is traditionally thought. Apologetics in Christianity can accurately be defined as the giving of a defense on any doctrine and to anyone. Scripture and logic both argue this case. Thus, contemporary apologetics is generally a field that has been narrowed down too much to align with how Scripture teaches the topic.

Ultimately, this conclusion can be made: Since the word "apologetics" comes from the Greek word that means "defense/to make a defense," it stands to reason that anytime someone *makes a defense*, by definition, they are *doing* apologetics regardless of what said defense is about or to whom the defense is presented.

So What?

It is all well and good to say that apologetics has been reduced too much in modern times, but why does it matter? Looking at apologetics from a broader perspective is important because it fills a significant gap in theology. Theology is, at its base, simply the study of God. The challenge is that one can be a theologian and be *wrong* about God. Additionally, one can be a theologian and not believe in God. For example, the "About" page of Harvard Divinity School's PhD program states, "Some of us are adherents of a religious tradition; others are not at all religious."[1] Many atheists and agnostics practice theology; whether it is done in an attempt to disprove God or because they find God/gods fascinating does not matter. There is such a thing as correct theology; and understanding that apologetics can be applied in theology itself is nothing but advantageous for Christian theologians. It means that we can use the same training and tactics that are used in defending the faith against outside ideologies to defend the faith against attacks from within Christianity, even if the attacks are unintentional. The truth of

---

1. "PhD Program," Harvard Divinity School, accessed July 8, 2024, https://hd s.harvard.edu/academics/degree-programs/phd-program .

the matter is that we regularly use apologetics within theology. This book has been written primarily to help readers under- stand this reality so that apologetics can be used as effectively as possible within theology. After all, it is difficult to properly learn or utilize something that one does not know needs to be learned or even can be used in a particular context.

Chapter 6

A Brief Call to Action

If you found value in this book, please consider leaving an honest review on your favorite book review site (Amazon, BookBub, Goodreads, etc.). Reviews are tremendously helpful to authors, and I highly appreciate each one that I receive.

Also, if you are an academic, why not consider joining me in this experiment to see if self-publishing journal articles in book form is a viable method for publishing? If it can catch on, it has the potential to revolutionize academic publishing. This is especially true if we can figure out how to develop a solid peer review process for self-published titles. I have some thoughts on how this might work, but I have not attempted anything yet and am open to ideas. If you want to know more about my process or would like to give me your ideas on peer review possibilities, please email me at ljandersonbooks@outl ook.com. I would want to make sure that the peer review is solid (double-blind ideally), that each publication is subject to some quality control before it gets to the reviewer so we aren't wasting people's time, and that there is some reliable way to signify that the article/book has been peer-reviewed.

My current thought on this is to use my publishing company Lamad Press LLC as a go-between for reviewers and authors who want to get their books peer-reviewed. Some type of statement with a unique identifier could be added to the copyright page of books that have successfully undergone a peer review. This would make peer review an *optional step* of publishing rather than a contractual obligation. Theoretically, it should be possible to publish article-length, original research as books without needing a formal peer review as they should be able to be sorted out post-publishing. Well-written, edited, and researched articles should rise to the top.

BIBLIOGRAPHY

Akin, Daniel L., David S. Dockery, Nathan A. Finn, and
Christopher W. Morgan, eds. *A Handbook of Theology*.
Nashville, TN: B&H Publishing Group, 2023.

Bernard, Ramm. "The Apologetic of the Old Testament:
The Basis of a Biblical and Christian Apologetic." *Bulletin of the Evangelical Theological Society* 1.4 (Fall
1958), 15-20.

Cowan, Steven B., and William Lane Craig. *Five Views on
Apologetics*. Grand Rapids, MI: Zondervan, 2000.

Dunn, James D. G. *The Theology of Paul the Apostle*. Grand
Rapids, MI: Wm. B. Eerdmans Publishing, 2006.

Elwell, Walter, and Robert Yarbrough. *Encountering the New Testament: A Historical and Theological Survey*. Grand Rapids, MI: Baker Academic, 2013.

Feinberg, John S. *No One Like Him: The Doctrine of God*. Wheaton, IL: Crossway, 2001.

Gould, Paul, Travis Dickenson, and R. Keith Loftin. *Stand Firm: Apologetics and the Brilliance of the Gospel*. Nashville, TN: B&H Academic, 2018.

Hammett, John S. *Biblical Foundations for Baptist Churches: A Contemporary Ecclesiology*. Grand Rapids, MI: Kregel Publications, 2005.

Moreland, J. P. *Love the Lord Your God With All Your Mind: The Role of Reason in the Life of the Soul*. Colorado Springs, CO: NavPress, 2012.

Nicolson, Stuart. "Original Apologetics." *Theology and Philosophy of Education* 2, no. 2 (Dec. 2023): 4-12.

Riecker, Siegbert. *The Old Testament Basis of Christian Apologetics: A Biblical-Theological Survey*. Eugene, OR: Wipf and Stock Publishers, 2018.

Wilson, Todd, and Gerald Hiestand, eds. *Becoming a Pastor Theologian: New Possibilities for Church Leadership*. Downers Grove, IL: InterVarsity Press, 2016.

Womack, Jonathan M., and Jerry Pillay. "From the Tower to the Pews: A Call for Academic Theology to Re-Engage with the Local Context." *Hervormde Teologiese Studies* 75, no. 4 (2019): 1-8.

Zachhuber, Johannes. "What is Theology? Historical and Systematic Reflections." *International Journal for the Study of the Christian Church*. 21, (2021): 198-211.

ALSO BY

L. J. ANDERSON

Books

Contending for the Truth: A Biblical Look at Eighteen Contentious Doctrines (coming soon!)

www.ingramcontent.com/pod-product-compliance
Lightning Source LLC
Chambersburg PA
CBHW051600120626
46551CB00013B/1608